J. W. Schenck

The Rescued Child

J. W. Schenck

The Rescued Child

ISBN/EAN: 9783337215590

Printed in Europe, USA, Canada, Australia, Japan

Cover: Foto ©Thomas Meinert / pixelio.de

More available books at **www.hansebooks.com**

THE RESCUED CHILD.

BY MRS. J. W. SCHENCK.

PUBLISHED BY THE
AMERICAN TRACT SOCIETY,
150 NASSAU-STREET, NEW YORK.

MANY on reading this little work, will perhaps think the opening scenes too marvellous to be true; but the writer wishes to assure her readers that these facts, substantially, actually occurred in one of our Eastern states.

ENTERED according to Act of Congress, in the year 1868, by the AMERICAN TRACT SOCIETY, in the Clerk's Office of the District Court of the United States for the Southern District of New York.

CONTENTS.

CHAPTER I.
The Policeman ---------------------------PAGE 5

CHAPTER II.
The Rescue---------------------------------- 15

CHAPTER III.
The Mother and Son --------------------------- 22

CHAPTER IV.
The Unamiable Daughter ------------------------- 30

CHAPTER V.
The New Home --------------------------------- 39

CHAPTER VI.
Mrs. Lacy's Illness ----------------------------- 48

CHAPTER VII.
A Call from the East ---------------------------- 53

CHAPTER VIII.
India 61

CHAPTER IX.
Little Eddie 69

CHAPTER X.
Changes 77

CHAPTER XI.
A Letter 87
Conclusion 94

THE RESCUED CHILD.

CHAPTER I.

THE POLICEMAN.

"OH, if I only had assistance!" These words were spoken by a police-officer, as he leaned against a tree in front of a small dilapidated house, in an unfrequented street, in the city of ——.

The hour was fast verging towards midnight, and notwithstanding the bitter cold of the atmosphere and the icy condition of the pavements, the excited watchman had kept this position for some time, listening to the cries of a small child, and the heavy blows that frequently broke the stillness of the desolate place.

As the words above-mentioned burst from his lips, a gentleman who was hurrying by paused, and hesitatingly asked, as he saw the star that shone upon the breast of the speaker,

"Do you need assistance, sir? Is any thing wrong in this quarter?"

"Wrong?" returned the policeman, "just listen to those blows, and hear that poor little child scream; I am certain there is villany there."

"Why not enter and put a stop to this brutality at once?" questioned the new-comer.

"I could, sir, without doubt, had I the assistance of some kind-hearted family. What I need most is a woman's sympathy and counsel."

"What are the circumstances of the

case, sir? I may perhaps know the person you need."

"It is cold, standing here; and as I can do nothing to-night, I will walk with you a block or two, and in a few words tell my story. That house is held by a negress, and is one of the vilest dens in this city; it is the resort of persons of all ages and colors, and has been under my eye for some time, on account of its bad reputation. About two weeks since, I discovered that, secreted in that house, and probably stolen by the woman who detains it, is a beautiful white female child about eighteen months old. I succeeded once in obtaining a glimpse of the poor little thing, and I can assure you a more beautiful babe never breathed. The woman secretes it if a stranger approaches; locks it alone in a small, cold room, if obliged to leave the premises; and cruelly abuses it whenever it is restless or wakeful at night. I have made excuses to enter to inspect the premises; but though I can hear it crying, in what is apparently a large closet where it is suddenly thrust for concealment, nothing will induce the woman to unlock the door and let me see her babe. I have no proof that the child has been stolen, and therefore cannot arrest her, but I am convinced that such is the case. Sir, I shudder at the horrible future of that beautiful child if left in that den; and I only wait to find a person willing to adopt or care for her, before I forcibly wrest her from the clutches of this fiend in human shape."

"Can it be possible," exclaimed the gentleman, "that such depravity actually exists in this quiet city? Poor little babe! what fearful hands has she fallen into! But, sir, I am quite sure I can point you to a lady who will assist you in this matter. Mrs. Lacy is noted for her benevolence and piety. She has wealth, and her heart is ever alive to sympathy with sorrow. She does not live in this place, but is now here for a few weeks, and boards in the same house where I reside. If you think best, I will speak to her of this case to-morrow morning; and if you will call at my place of business at ten o'clock, I will let you know the result of our conversation."

"Thank you, sir; I should be much obliged to you if you will thus assist me. I confess I would like to rescue that suffering child."

After a few words more, during which the address of the gentleman was carefully noted, the two bade each other good-night, and separated.

At the hour appointed the next day,

the kind-hearted policeman presented himself at the store of Mr. Clay, who had conversed with him the night before. As soon as his stout form and honest face appeared within the doorway, Mr. Clay advanced cordially to meet him, exclaiming with animation as he did so:

"I am so glad you are punctual, for I have good news awaiting your attention. Mrs. Lacy was, as I felt sure she would be, deeply interested in that poor little one. So much did her kind heart yearn towards the innocent child, that she decided to see you herself, this morning. You will please step back with me into the office, and I will introduce you to my friend."

Following the steps of Mr. Clay, the policeman crossed the store, and was ushered into a private office, neatly furnished, where sat a noble-looking woman about forty years of age, whose countenance was a true index of amiability, benevolence, and refinement.

"Mrs. Lacy, this is Mr. Hardcastle, the policeman we spoke of this morning," said Mr. Clay, as he offered the good man a chair.

"I am glad to meet you, madam," remarked Mr. Hardcastle, "and if your womanly feelings can be interested in the rescue of a sweet little child from sorrow, I shall be truly delighted. Had I a wife and family I should not have asked assistance; but I have lost all these home treasures by death, and am compelled to look to strangers for sympathy."

"You have no idea, I am told, whose child this is, nor how she came to be in the possession of this old negress," said Mrs. Lacy.

"Not the slightest. But it is a beautiful child; its skin is as pure white as ever met your eye. I am certain that she never came honestly by her. My opinion is, that the child has been stolen. I much wish to find a person willing to care for her. As soon as this is accomplished, I will go to the house, demand the child, and if not immediately surrendered, will search the premises, take it from its concealment, and carry it to the place of refuge immediately."

"Mr. Hardcastle, do so as soon as possible, and I will take charge of it. I have means enough, and can give you every satisfactory reference as to respectability, and you need not feel anxious about its probable future. I do not say I will adopt it, as I have children of my own; but I will certainly provide for it, and see that it has the best of care. Perhaps, if I am pleased with her appearance and disposition upon trial, I may eventually receive her as my own, but this remains to be seen. I make no promise that binds me to that course, but I do promise to care for her, and see that she is properly and piously reared."

"Thank you, over and over again, dear madam; that is all we can reasonably require. I will merely say, that looks greatly deceive, if she does not soon find a way into your heart, and become as one of your own," returned the honest policeman.

"We shall see; time alone can determine. But, Mr. Hardcastle, whatever you think best to do must be done speedily, as I leave this place day after to-morrow, for my own residence, and must take the child with me if I have her at all. I merely came to this city to place my son in college, and see him settled in a good home. This having been accomplished, I must speedily return. Can you bring the babe to No. —— —— street, to-morrow?"

"I can, and perhaps sooner. I will, if possible, effect an entrance this afternoon. If so, and I succeed, shall I bring the child at once to you?"

"Certainly; I will remain at home till I see you, so that there can be no trouble. Poor little creature! I shall count the hours until I have her clasped in my arms."

Tears stood in the dark eyes of the lady as she uttered these words; and as Mr. Hardcastle noticed them, he felt a thrill of genuine satisfaction, for he was sure that a tender heart awaited the poor little stranger.

CHAPTER II.

The Rescue.

"Inasmuch as ye have done it unto one of the least of these, ye have done it unto me."

ABOUT five hours later in the day, a carriage drove to the door of a large boarding-house, on —— street, and a person wearing the uniform of a policeman, and bearing in his arms an infant, around which an old faded shawl was wrapped, descended, and passing quickly within the door, was ushered directly into the presence of Mrs. Lacy.

"Dear madam, I have brought you the sweetest little pearl you ever saw: Look!" exclaimed he as, placing his burden upon her lap, he threw back the covering, and exposed to view a perfect picture of infantile loveliness.

Mrs. Lacy uttered an exclamation of delight as she gazed upon the babe. Its skin was beautifully white, its eyes a dark deep blue, while its golden hair lay in tiny ringlets over a well-shaped head. Its mouth was almost like a rosebud, so beautiful and fresh were its lovely curves, and the baby-laugh that greeted her ear as she first gazed into its face fairly won her motherly heart.

"She is indeed a little beauty, Mr. Hardcastle; but how did you manage to rescue her?"

"I went directly to the house, about an hour ago, accompanied by a brother officer, and passing into a side gate, we went to the rear of the dwelling, and opening the back door which fortunately was unfastened, walked in and faced the woman, before she could realize our presence. The poor little babe was sobbing by itself in a dirty cradle, while the negress was working around, heedless of its tears. The moment her eyes met mine, she darted to the cradle, and attempted to seize the child; but I was too quick for her, for springing forward and seizing her arm, I held her back, while I demanded an explanation of her having in her possession a white child.

"Laws! 't a'n't none of your bizness I guess," she answered spitefully. "I cum honestly by it, I tell you!"

"That I very much doubt. Where is the child's mother?" returned I.

"Dead and buried, and she guv me the child wid her dying breff."

"What induced her to give it to you? Why not place it among people of her own color?"

"'Cause she did n't, that's all I know

'bout it; see here, mister, you let go of my arm, and clear out; this is my house, and that child belongs to me."

"No, it does not! There you are mistaken!" returned I. "It is my property now. The law demands that she be taken from this vile den."

"You touch that baby if you dare!" shouted the enraged negress, as she aimed a furious blow at my face, but I dodged it, and it missed its mark. My companion then came to my assistance, and with his help I secured her in a chair, and then proceeded to search the premises, to discover even one little clue to its parentage.

"And did you find the least relic?" anxiously inquired Mrs. Lacy.

"Only this little gold necklace with the initials upon the clasp, B. D., and this note, evidently written by some well-educated man."

"To Molly Clarkson:

"I send you with this, the amount due for the board of that baby. Such a whining as the parents keep up about the loss of the brat, is a great treat for me. Ah, they have rued the day when they dared to cross my path. Keep dark, feed the brat well, and when I return from the journey I am about taking, I shall see you and learn how you have succeeded in your mission. Woe betide you, if my game slip through your fingers! Remember!"

"The infamous wretch!" exclaimed Mrs. Lacy, as she read the paper, to which no date or name was attached. "Surely we have clear evidence here that the babe was stolen from its parents solely for revenge. But what did you do with the woman?"

"After I had obtained the child," continued Mr. Hardcastle, "and released her from her chair, her rage knew no bounds! She raved and stamped, flew at us with all her fury, endeavoring to drag the child from my arms; but the weight of Smith's club made her calm down a little, and while he marched her off to the 'stone-jug,' as we call the lock-up here, I took the little one in my arms and drove to this place. I think, madam, that the more private we keep the story, the less likely the writer of that wicked note will be to track our movements. I am glad you do not reside here; but where is your home, if I may inquire?"

"In Edgeville, a beautiful country village, but which I can readily reach by the public conveyances; and I will leave to-morrow, if I can secure comfortable travelling clothes for the baby by that time, as you see these filthy rags afford neither warmth nor covering. But did the negress tell you its name?"

"Not she! I could not induce her to breathe it; and as the darling cannot talk, you will be obliged to give her a name yourself."

Mrs. Lacy mused a moment, and then exclaimed: "Her first name at all events shall be the one you gave her, little Pearl. Her skin is so snowy white, there could be nothing more appropriate!"

The man smiled, and as he bent over the babe before departing, these words fell from his honest lips:

"God bless you, sweet little Pearl."

It was the first blessing that came as a ray of hope, to illumine the future of the rescued child. May the echoes of that prayer ever reverberate around the home and heart of the little pilgrim as she journeys on towards heaven.

"God bless you, sweet little Pearl."

CHAPTER III.

THE MOTHER AND SON.

"ERNEST, my son," said Mrs. Lacy, as the hour for their evening meal approached, and she heard the footsteps of her son passing through the hall on his way to his own room.

"Yes, mother, in one moment I will be with you," replied a voice from the hall, as the speaker ran lightly up the stairs to the floor above.

Mrs. Lacy closed the door again, and smiled as she glanced towards the bed, where her eyes rested upon the curling golden ringlets that just appeared above the snow-white spread; for little Pearl was there, sleeping sweetly.

"Oh, I hope my children will not be displeased with this infringement upon their rights," she silently murmured, as she sank into a chair without noticing the entrance of her son; and the word "Mother" only called her attention to the speaker.

Ernest Lacy was about sixteen years of age, and was a fair specimen of fast approaching manhood. Tall and finely moulded was this first-born of our friend, although his easy manners betokened a perfect unconsciousness of any such fact. In character he bid fair to be all that was excellent, having ever been a devoted son, a tender brother, and a faithful friend. Undeviating in his principles, moral in his habits, and of late truly pious, he had gradually become his mother's helper and adviser, as well as her greatest comfort in her widowhood and loneliness.

"Ernest, do you remember our conversation this morning, in reference to that poor little babe?"

"Yes, mother, I have scarcely thought of any thing else all day," he replied.

"Well, my son, the little girl is here."

"Here, mother; where?" exclaimed the surprised youth, glancing hastily around the room. Before she could reply, his eyes rested upon the golden rings upon the pillow, and crossing the floor, he gently raised the covers, and fairly started back with surprise at the charming picture before him.

"How beautiful!" he exclaimed, as his mother glided to his side, and laid her hand tenderly upon his arm. "She is a perfect cherub, and looks more like wax than a living child."

"Then you are not displeased, Ernest, at another looking to me for protection?"

"Displeased? Never. How could you conscientiously do otherwise, when you have those written words to guide you in the right path: 'Inasmuch as ye did it not to one of the least of these, ye did it not to me.' No, mother, I am not displeased; I am proud to have you accomplish so charitable an act. I will assist you in watching over her."

"'Little Pearl,' that is the name I told the good policeman I would call her," interposed the mother.

"Shall the other name be Lacy?"

"No, my son; I have not exactly adopted her. I do not think it best to do that now. We will give her another fancy name. Can you think of any?"

"Courtenay, Fitzgerald! No; both are too romantic. Stanley, Woodford—"

"Stop; you need go no farther. I like the last you mentioned," returned Mrs. Lacy.

"Woodford, Pearl Woodford. Yes, that sounds well. Let us then decide to leave it so," replied the young man. "Ah, little Pearl, we will take the best care of you, my birdie. Mother, it is a pity you broke up housekeeping now, is it not?"

"Rather; yet it enables me to perform a double charity. Our pastor at Edgeville is none too well cared for. I am almost certain Mrs. Colman and he would be glad to take this darling under their charge, as I will amply repay them for the trouble. She will then be where I can see her daily, and still benefit a Christian family."

"Your plan is admirable, dear mother; I trust you will find Mr. Colman willing, as certainly the little Pearl could never be in better hands."

"I am glad you think well of the arrangement. In a few years I shall probably resume housekeeping, and then if we find little Pearl an amiable, obedient child, the understanding must be, that they resign her into my own hands."

"What do you think Mattie will say, mother, to this new charge?" asked Ernest, after a long silence.

Mrs. Lacy sighed before she answered the question, and a painful shadow seemed to float over her face as she thoughtfully replied:

"Ah, Ernest, I am anxious about Mattie, she is so peculiar; from her I expect my only trouble."

Was that a prophecy? Can it be that even now, when the sunlight is breaking through the cloud that has enveloped the horizon of the baby-girl, can it be that a speck, a shadow, is looming up from the distance, and will it darken the future life of poor little Pearl?

The next day found Mrs. Lacy at the

dépôt, on her way to N——, whence a few hours' ride would bring her to Edgeville. The sweet face of the beautiful babe was concealed as much as possible from prying eyes, by the thick folds of the veil that was wrapped over its warm new hood, while the tender arms of Mrs. Lacy encircled its fragile form.

Ernest did not leave the side of his mother and her little charge, until he had placed her in a rather retired seat; and even then he lingered until the warning was given, that obliged him to say farewell.

"Good-by, dear mother and little Pearl. Don't forget to write every particular of your reception at home, for I shall long to hear."

So whispered the affectionate boy as he left her side, and sprang from the train; then as his light step glided over the snowy paths of the college grounds, his thoughts went on with the devoted mother; while the innocent, beautiful baby face of little Pearl often danced before his eyes that day, as he bent over his tasks, in the time-honored walls of the glorious old institution, where so many of his youthful hours were to be spent, and where he hoped, by diligence and application, to please the many hearts that were fondly waiting his success.

CHAPTER IV.

The Unamiable Daughter.

WE will not linger to enter into details of the journey, which was safely accomplished by our friend, but will pass on to her arrival in the beautiful village of Edgeville. She descended from the carriage, passed at once to her own room, and was apparently much pleased to find it vacant.

"This is most fortunate," she said to herself. "I am glad Mattie is still at school, as it gives me time to rest, and to make little Pearl look as pretty as possible."

Hastily throwing off her outer garments she opened a large closet and from the capacious depths of a timeworn trunk, took out article after article of a little girl's tiny wardrobe.

"Ah, Mattie, how lovely you were, when my eager hands arrayed your wee form in these garments! Now we will see how they become my little Pearl, after lying useless so many years."

It took but a few moments to re-robe the little creature; and the joyful smile that wreathed the lips of the lady as her task was completed, told of the utmost satisfaction at the looks of little Pearl, as she stood folded in fine needle-work, with gay ribbons looping the sleeves and encircling her waist.

Mrs. Lacy caught the lovely babe to her bosom and kissed enthusiastically its little face, after long contemplating the pleasing effect of her newly acquired wardrobe.

"My God," she murmured, "I thank

thee that I have been enabled to snatch this darling from the clutches of that wicked woman. May she ever be a blessing to my home."

She paused, for at that instant, two arms were twined around her neck, and the lips of a dark-eyed girl of fourteen were pressed upon her own.

"Why, mother, when did you come home, and how did you leave Ernest? A collegian by this time, I suppose. But who is this?" added the young girl, as her eyes for the first time wandered to the floor and rested upon the baby, who now sat upon the carpet, playing with a pretty toy that had also emerged from the above-mentioned trunk.

"Sit down, daughter, and I will answer all your questions. I arrived about an hour since, and am delighted to see my child again and looking so bright and blooming; Ernest is now a fresh-

THE UNAMIABLE DAUGHTER.

man in classical halls, well, happy, and finely settled; and this is little Pearl Woodford, a friendless child that I have taken under my protection and into my affections. I hope you will love her, as she has no other ties that we know of."

"I shall do no such thing! Love a little pauper brat! not I, indeed! I do not see what you brought her here for," angrily retorted the young girl, her dark eyes flashing with indignation and her lip curling with scorn.

"Mattie, restrain yourself: I took her because I felt it to be my duty, and in obedience to my Master's command when he said, 'Feed my lambs.'"

"Pshaw! You always have some Bible to bring up! Where did you pick up the brat, anyhow?"

"My daughter, if you cannot speak more respectfully, be silent. Remember, I desire you to be kind to this child, and on no account to apply to it again the contemptuous term you have already twice uttered, under pain of my deepest displeasure. I obtained the child while absent, and intend to rear her with the same care I have ever lavished upon you. I shall educate her well, and provide for her in every respect. No opposition on your part will prevent it, and the less you say the better you will appear."

Mrs. Lacy turned to her writing-desk, as she finished speaking, and hastily penned a note to her pastor, asking the favor of an interview that afternoon at her rooms. As she traced the words upon the paper, she did not see the hateful look upon the face of her child, nor the bitter angry expression flashing in her eyes, as she fastened a malignant glance upon the inoffensive little one.

"She will repent the day she brought her here before very long, if I have my way," she muttered, as her mother left the room a moment to despatch a messenger with her note to the parsonage. "Love a beggarly chit like that? Not I, indeed! Mother grows stranger every day. She does not seem to have one grain of true family pride. The idea of taking a pauper to her bosom, instead of sending her to the almshouse where she belongs!"

Here the angry girl fairly stamped her foot in a rage, while her vehemence frightened the little one, causing low sobs to issue from her lips, and large tears to roll over her cheeks. "Ah, cry on, little beggar, for all me," exclaimed the unamiable Mattie, crossing to the farther side of the room, and throwing herself upon a lounge, when one kind word would have soothed the baby's grief.

"Mattie, I am astonished at you,"

said Mrs. Lacy, as she re-entered the apartment; "could you not have amused little Pearl one moment in my absence?"

"Not I, indeed, she might cry until doomsday, before I would soil my fingers with her ladyship."

Mrs. Lacy looked sternly at her rebellious child; then taking Pearl in her arms, she kissed her rosy lips, and soon by her fond caresses restored the usual smiles and dimples.

That afternoon, Mr. Colman had a long interview with Mrs. Lacy, and seemed deeply interested in the story which that lady told him, in strict confidence, of the child's rescue from the negress. Mr. Colman agreed with her in the opinion, that it was not advisable to inform a single person, not even Mattie, of her real history; fearing that the villanous man who had evidently been the chief mover in snatching her from the arms of her parents, should trace her hither.

"But," he asked anxiously during the course of their conversation, "shall you not endeavor to find the parents, who are even yet, according to this note that you have allowed me to read, mourning for their lost darling?"

"I shall, through the police-officer, Mr. Hardcastle. I gave him ample funds to advertise it in all the leading papers of the day; application for information to be made to him. All we can now do, is to wait for an answer."

' Well, Mrs. Lacy, with Mrs. Colman's consent, I will gladly take the little girl to our home and heart. I will speak to my wife immediately; and if she approves, which I do not doubt, we will both return in a short time and take her before dark to our home."

"Thank you, dear Mr. Coleman. I

shall rest contented if I only know that she is at home in so love-girdled and sunny a spot as the parsonage."

In a short time Mr. Colman returned with his kind-hearted wife, to whom little Pearl instinctively turned as to an old friend; and much to Mrs. Lacy's satisfaction, the arrangement was fully completed, and the beautiful babe was that night sleeping close to the bed-side of Mrs. Colman in a crib provided by her kind benefactress, Mrs. Lacy.

CHAPTER V.

THE NEW HOME.

THE home to which Pearl Woodford had been introduced by the kindness of her benefactress could in no wise be excelled for piety, comfort, and kindness. Mr. and Mrs. Colman having no children, the baby-girl immediately filled a niche in their house long unsupplied; and her beauty and pretty ways soon caused them to regard her with a parent's true and tender affection. She was indeed as a ray of sunlight to the toil-worn pastor and his wife. She was such a good and pleasant babe that they could not but love her, and her coming brought them so little extra trouble that they never had cause to repine.

For hours she would sit upon the floor surrounded by her playthings, no sound save now and then a silvery laugh issuing from her lips; while often she would play on until her eyelids would droop, and Mrs. Colman would be surprised to find her asleep, one hand grasping a gay worsted ball, and the other a brightly-dressed doll, while her golden head rested upon the sides of a woolly toy-sheep.

No mother could have surveyed this innocent and pretty picture with greater fondness than did Mrs. Colman; and gliding to the study-door, she would not be content until her husband stood by her side to sympathize with her feelings of fond delight.

Twice every week a maid appeared

at the parsonage to carry the little one to the rooms of Mrs. Lacy, to spend the morning with that kind lady; and ever upon her return would her tiny hands be filled with gifts with which to amuse' herself until they met again.

As months passed on, Mrs. Lacy found that the gentleness and amiability of her pet had won no small place in the domain of her heart, and she looked upon her now with much of the same motherly love she bore for her own. Ernest, also, during his brief trips to his native village, found the darling golden-headed baby a source of great pleasure and a willing sharer in many a frolic.

But Mattie still remained obdurate. No kind word had ever escaped her in regard to the child. No caresses ever fell upon its white brow from her cold lips; but bitter reproaches alone greeted her mother's ear for her growing partiality to a pauper child, as she ever persisted in styling her protégé.

Poor Mrs. Lacy grieved sadly over her daughter's stubborn and uncharitable disposition. It was a constant source of sorrow to her tender, loving heart, which, could Mattie have reflected upon it, she would have seen and avoided. Children little know the anguish of parents in view of their shortcomings. They little realize that their selfish and disobedient conduct is as a sharp knife to the hearts that love them best, as well as a deep offence to their ever-watchful heavenly Father.

Time passed swiftly on, and as the child improved, and words came to her aid, and her tiny feet found their proper use, it seemed to her loving friends that the little wayside blossom became more and more attractive and engaging; and as no answer had ever been returned to the widespread advertisements that had been published in regard to her, they felt that she was now really their own, to bring up and train as they wished. and they blessed God that they had the will to endeavor to bring her up for his glory.

In former days, previous to his settlement in Edgeville, Mr. Colman and his wife had been missionaries to India, where they had labored acceptably for eight years; when the health of this devoted servant of God drooped, and in order to save his life, he was directed to return to America for rest and restoration. For one year after his arrival he had been so prostrated that it was impossible to labor at all in his Master's vineyard; but after that time a gradual improvement became perceptible; he accepted a call to the church at Edgeville, and there by his energy and earnestness in the cause of Christ he won the affections of a warm-hearted people. Of course, after such a personal knowledge of the ignorance and sinfulness of the heathen, the thoughts of this devoted couple often wandered to their former field of labor, and their conversation referred very frequently to the manners and customs of the degraded people once their peculiar care.

Little Pearl, from her babyhood, listened with the deepest interest to these accounts; and no story could interest her loving heart so deeply, after the story of her Saviour's coming and dying upon earth to save even little children, as the interesting accounts of scenes that had transpired in that far-off land.

"Tell me a story, auntie," was ever the pleading wish of the little one.

"What shall it be, my birdie?" would be the reply of the good woman as she raised her to her lap, and pressed her hand caressingly over her golden hair.

"Something about the poor little boys and girls that have no Saviour."

Then, when a description would be given of the Hindoo mother throwing her babe into the Ganges, and the wicked Khonds cutting the flesh from the bones of living children to appease their gods by such fearful sacrifices of cruelty and blood, tears of sympathy and horror would flow over her little cheeks, and she would exclaim:

"Oh, dear auntie, will not God let me go, when I am old enough, to tell them about our blessed Jesus? Will he not let me save the lives of some of these poor little things?"

"Yes, Pearl, if you really wish it *then*, probably he will allow you to become a missionary."

"But what shall I do to help them

before that time comes, auntie, so many will be dead then that are living now? Can I do any thing now?"

"Yes, my child, you can pray that good people may go to them, and you can still give part of the money mamma Lacy gives you so freely to send them God's holy word."

"I have done both these so long, auntie, that I should like something new."

"Very likely; but, Pearl, the heathen are there still, and daily prayers are necessary, and money must be sent all the time, or the missionaries cannot live, and the Bible cannot be given them," replied Mrs. Colman.

"Dear auntie, I did not mean to stop praying, neither did I intend to keep back my money, only I should like to be doing something to prepare me for going by-and-by."

"Well, dear, how would you like to

learn to speak their language? That would be getting ready very fast."

"Would it, auntie? Then let us begin to-day. You will teach me, will you not? And you remember I have caught some words from uncle and you already."

"Yes, Pearl, that would be quite an assistance."

So, notwithstanding little Pearl was only seven years old, every day she tried to learn a little of the heathen language; and being very quick at committing to memory, and her memory being very retentive, it was remarkable what progress she made in mastering the simple words her kind instructress selected to teach and amuse her.

CHAPTER VI.

Mrs. Lacy's Illness.

THIS dear little girl did not neglect learning to read her own mother-tongue, while she strove to remember what she heard of this heathen language; for at three years of age she could spell words of one syllable, and now at seven she read distinctly and well. From her babyhood she had shown she had fine talents, and Mrs. Colman often was obliged to take away her book, fearing that such application in her early years would injure her health; and now so eager was she to do something like missionary work, that Mrs. Colman could scarcely control her in her eager haste to learn the meaning of the strange-sounding words often spoken in the family.

Mrs. Lacy was greatly surprised one day, when Pearl was passing the morning with her, to hear the little one go from article to article around, and call each one by the name Mrs. Colman had taught her.

"Why, Pearl, what is that you are saying?" she asked finally, as the child had placed "Daisy," her doll, upon a chair; and with blue eyes sparkling and little hands gesturing with excitement she stood before her, pouring out something that seemed incomprehensible nonsense to the matter-of-fact woman.

"Why, mamma Lacy"—for thus her benefactress had taught her to call her—"don't you know? I am making believe that Daisy is a poor little Hindoo child, and I was trying to tell her about Jesus."

"But what language is Daisy supposed to understand?"

"The language the people speak where uncle was."

"But can you talk it?"

"Just a little bit, mamma. Auntie is teaching me, and I can say a few words now."

"But why do you want to talk like the heathen? What possible good can it do you?"

"O mamma, so much, so very much; for I am going to be a missionary when I grow up; so when I get to India I must know how to speak their words, or I could not tell them how Jesus died to save their souls," replied Pearl.

"Is it possible," thought Mrs. Lacy, "that this thing can ever be? Have I indeed rescued one of Jesus' lambs for so great and glorious a work? Who but God alone knows what good may yet be accomplished by this sweet and pious child?"

Yes; Mrs. Lacy was right when she called Pearl a pious child; for from the time she could lisp her baby words her heart was alive to the love of Jesus. The very thoughts of this little girl seemed to be sincere and lovely. Often her tiny form was found kneeling alone in prayer when her friends knew that something had occurred to vex or disappoint her; and then, relieved by prayer, she would return with her sweet face radiant as the very impersonation of love and peace.

When little Pearl was about twelve and a half years of age, the health of Mrs. Lacy began to give way, and serious apprehensions were felt as to her recovery. So rapid seemed the decline that her physicians recommended an immediate trip to Europe as most likely to benefit her, and Ernest made hasty preparations to accompany his mother and Mattie.

The beautiful place which they had bought and occupied about two years before, was rented to a careful couple without children; and as Pearl was such a comfort to Mr. and Mrs. Colman, it was decided to leave her still at the parsonage.

Pearl seemed deeply affected at the serious illness of her friend; and when the last kiss of farewell was given, she clung to her neck with sobs of anguish.

"Good-by, darling mamma Lacy; God will take care of you, for Pearl will ask him to every day."

Mrs. Lacy kissed her rosy lips with tearful eyes, then handed her to Ernest, who caressed his pet fondly in bidding her adieu; and so they parted.

CHAPTER VII.

A Call from the East.

ABOUT six months after Mrs. Lacy's departure, Mr. Colman received a letter which made quite a stir in his quiet home, and would probably cause many changes in his household. For several days after its receipt, both husband and wife appeared to be in deep reflection, and spent many hours in fervent conversation and prayer.

The cause of this unrest was an earnest call for help from the station in India where he had formerly labored; a stirring appeal that he would, if restored to health, come back to assist in their labor of love. "Come back," wrote his brother missionaries, "Come back, and help us. You and your wife, with your knowledge of the language, your love for perishing souls, your earnest zeal in the cause of Christ, are the very ones we pray for and long to welcome. Brother, sister in the Lord, does not this call find such an answering chord in your own hearts, that it will induce you to make the sacrifice, and listen once more to the urgent appeals of your far-off friends?"

After long and deliberate reflection, it became evident to this pious couple that it was their duty to obey this call of Providence, and once more become laborers in the foreign missionary field. But one obstacle presented itself, and that was the presence of little Pearl; and the trust reposed in them by Mrs. Lacy, who was to remain some time in Italy, as that climate seemed to be most beneficial to her health.

A CALL FROM THE EAST.

One day the subject was accidentally spoken of in the presence of Pearl, and both were amazed at the earnestness of her pleading that they should go at once to the poor, dying heathen, *and take her with them.*

"O dear uncle," she exclaimed, with tears in her eyes; "you surely will not refuse to let me go. You know I have always said I should be a missionary. I know some of the language now, enough to talk to the little ones, and I have prayed so long that God would let me go to these ignorant people. Uncle, if you do decide to go, you will surely take your Pearl."

"Dear child, I would gladly take you, but mamma Lacy might not like it."

"I told her a long time before she went away," returned Pearl, "that God was going to make me a missionary when I grew up. Pray, let me go, dear uncle, I may never grow up. I can do some good I am sure to the children, and I know mamma will not object."

"Well, Pearl, I will write and consult with her about it."

"May I write a little bit also, and ask her for myself?" said the little girl eagerly.

"You may, my darling; but you must commence immediately, as I shall soon be ready to write my own letter."

Away bounded little Pearl to seek her auntie and write her letter, which shows how anxious this dear child was to do something for Jesus.

"My own dear Mamma: As uncle says I may write a letter and send with his, I am going to hurry as fast as possible to get it ready, so that I need not keep him waiting. Dear mamma, I have such a very great favor to ask of you, and I am so anxious to have you consent to it. Uncle will tell you that he thinks of going back to India as a missionary, and I wish very much to go with him. I feel so sorry for those poor people who have no Bible and no Jesus to love, and I want to carry them the good news that Jesus died to take them to heaven; and perhaps they will believe it, if they see a little girl come so far to teach them this. I could talk a little to them now, auntie says; I know now so many words used by them. Mamma Lacy, let me go, and I will always be thankful to you, and God will love you for it too. I cannot write any more now. With much love to brother Ernest and Mattie, I am ever your own little girl.

"PEARL WOODFORD."

Mr. Colman's letter was longer and more definite. He explained to his absent friend the considerations that had induced himself and Mrs. Colman to think it their duty to return to their former field of labor, and left it with her to decide what should be done with Pearl; expressing, at the same time, their deep anxiety to take the child with them, and Pearl's great desire not to be separated from them. He told Mrs. Lacy how the little girl had prayed to become a missionary, using all her feeble endeavors to fit herself for this work, and now, how she implored them to allow her to accompany them. He closed his letter by urging an immediate reply, promising, if she consented to her going, to take the most faithful charge of her; to watch over her health, and in case she drooped, to return her to Mrs. Lacy's fostering care whenever an opportunity offered."

Some time elapsed before a letter was received in reply, and then as it was handed to Mr. Colman, Pearl turned deadly pale with the excitement and the fear that her request had been denied.

To her great joy, however, it contained Mrs. Lacy's consent, as her health continued too precarious for her to return to take charge of her.

"I know, my dear pastor, your affection for our little girl, and your devoted love to the cause of Christ. I am perfectly satisfied to leave her with you wherever you go, and to commend you both to the kind care of our heavenly Father. That Pearl will be a comfort to you when far away from your native land I well know; and that she may be of some service to the ignorant and perishing heathen children, is my fervent prayer. I shall still continue to send her ample spending-money, and yourself the yearly allowance I have always made you, in return for your labor of love towards my darling. In case of my death, my will provides handsomely for her future; and you also, kind friend, are there remembered. God bless you and your wife in this great undertaking. I would that I could see you before you sail, that I might bid you farewell, and fold my precious Pearl once more to my bosom. Dear child! dearer now than ever to my heart; may Jesus watch over her and guard her for ever. Farewell.

"OLIVE M. LACY."

CHAPTER VIII.

India.

ALL alone on the broad, deep ocean, the noble ship "Flying Fawn" was proudly sailing, cleaving the foam-crested waves, now riding high on a rolling billow, then darting with a swift, bold plunge deep into a yawning chasm that opened below.

On board that vessel bound for "India's coral strand," were the Rev. Mr. Colman, his wife, and little Pearl Woodford. Though in the first part of their voyage they were dreadfully sea-sick, yet they were patient and hopeful during it all. At length the stately ship had been over four months on the rolling deep, and was fast nearing their desired haven.

What a happy and blessed thing it is, after a season of danger and trial, to know that the haven of our hopes is close at hand. Thus is it with all Christians; they have been tossing about on the sea of life for many years, yet at its close they rejoice, for the harbor of heaven is but a little way off, and soon, very soon, they will be safely anchored there.

I will not linger to describe the arrival of our wanderers at their distant home, nor the joyful welcome that awaited them at the station to which they repaired.

Pearl was amazed at almost every thing she saw: the strange manners and customs of the natives and their uncouth appearance; the very expression of their faces filled her with awe and dread.

But she soon became accustomed to the change, and her heart overflowed with joy at the efforts the servants of God were constantly making for the benefit of the poor deluded beings around them.

Mr. Colman found that great progress had been made since he left the mission. Many conversions had taken place, and now quite a number of native Christians gathered in the comfortable buildings that had been constructed for their use. The mission houses were also comfortable, and Mr. Colman soon felt at home in the one set apart for the use of his family.

Both he and his wife went heartily and eagerly to work, instructing those that came for instruction, and conversing gladly with inquirers anxious on account of their sins.

The schools were large and flourishing, and in them little Pearl seemed perfectly happy. She would gather the dusky children about her, and often, hour after hour, her little tongue would run as fast as her limited knowledge of the native language would permit; and her favorite theme seemed to be the preciousness of the Saviour.

The children soon became deeply attached to "the little teacher," as they called her, and were never so contented as when listening to the artless words of this pious, loving girl. Many of these little children were so won by her earnestness and persuasive powers, that they very early became disciples of Jesus, and their influence over others was of the utmost service.

But I must tell you something of the strange gods Pearl saw worshipped in that benighted land.

In India alone, there are said to be

three hundred and thirty millions of gods, of which one called Brahm has the first place in their estimation. They style him the "Supreme Being," but yet never worship him, as he is supposed to be always fast asleep. In the place of Brahm the natives worship a multitude of smaller gods. But drawn from the essence of Brahm are three great gods, called Brumha, Vishnoo, and Siva.

Then besides these, there is in one part of India, near Orissa, a very celebrated god, called Juggernaut, which word means, "the Lord of the world." Vast multitudes of people go every year to worship this idol. Sometimes they go great distances, performing the whole journey by rolling on the ground. Thousands of people die on the way, and one writer says "that for many miles around it, the roads are strewed with the bones and skulls of the poor pilgrims. Dogs, jackals, and vultures live on their dead bodies."

Sometimes Juggernaut is placed on a great car, with enormous wheels, and poor deluded creatures lie down and allow these wheels to pass over their bodies, thus crushing them to death. Then again, large crowds gather themselves around the temple of this god, to win his favor by torturing their own bodies in a most dreadful manner.

It is the constant work of the missionaries in India to endeavor to enlighten these poor Hindoos, and to induce them to throw aside these senseless idols, by telling them of the one only living and true God, and Jesus Christ his Son. Oh, how they work and strive and pray, far away in that distant land, for this great object; and that the Holy Spirit may help them in this labor of love, and many souls be brought to God through their instrumentality, should ever be the petition of all true Christians.

Many a blessing has attended their work in answer to prayer, and even now, many a Hindoo has been converted, and having died, is singing the praises of God in heaven. Will not the little girls and boys who live in our own dear country pray for the blessing of God upon this holy work?

Little Pearl prayed much for these poor, ignorant creatures, and she worked too, by talking to the children of the sinfulness of the practices they had been taught to believe so meritorious. She told them often, that killing themselves would never win a smile from Juggernaut, for he was only a piece of painted wood; but that trusting in and loving Jesus who died for them upon the cross, would win the favor of the one almighty God, and obtain a sure passport to heaven. Sometimes this would make them very angry, and after stoutly contradicting her they would sullenly run away, and not come near her again for days; but a childish curiosity to hear more of the pretty stories she told would overcome their temper, and they would gradually approach again, to listen and wonder at things so new and strange.

Then Pearl, who had ever shown a great taste for music, could sing very pretty hymns of praise to Jesus. The children, with all their ignorance, were charmed by sweet sounds; and as she sang, often quite a number would draw near to listen. These opportunities the little girl seldom allowed to pass without closing by some story or word that would impress their minds or touch their feelings. In this way, even so young a child accomplished much.

CHAPTER IX.

LITTLE EDDIE.

ONE day Pearl had accompanied Mr. and Mrs. Colman in a walk some little distance from their residence, and in quite an unfrequented spot they were startled by hearing low moans issue from a clump of bushes not far off; and as no one was then in sight, Mr. Colman parted the leaves and looked in.

Lying there, alone and suffering, was a little native boy about four years of age. His features were pretty, and his large black eyes, as they were raised to the missionary, wore a pleading wretched look he could not withstand. The child had evidently been brought there sick, and left by some heartless wretch to die, alone and neglected by the wayside. He must have revived and crawled into these bushes, in his misery and despair, to escape from the vultures, which had already torn great pieces of flesh from his poor little arms.

Pearl burst into a passion of tears, as she beheld these bleeding wounds, and she besought her kind friends to take the little fellow home.

"I will help take care of him, auntie, and I will tell him if he lives, all about Jesus. Wont you take him, uncle, and let me call him mine?"

Knowing as he did that the little boy had been deserted for ever by his own friends, Mr. Colman spoke kindly to him, and wrapping him tenderly from observation in Mrs. Colman's shawl, they carried him away; and finally succeeded in taking him safely to the shelter of the mission.

That evening, after the poor child's wounds had been carefully attended to, and its sufferings so much relieved by some soothing anodyne that he had fallen into a gentle sleep, Pearl ventured to inquire of her uncle if he thought the parents would come for their child.

"I am quite sure they will not, my dear," replied the good man, "as I think when they left him in that desolate place, it was parting with him for ever."

"But supposing he revived after they left him, and recovered, would they not then carry him back to their home, if they found it out?"

"No, darling, I am quite sure that they would never again receive him. Into the river Ganges, which, you know, is worshipped by the Hindoos as a sacred stream, mothers often throw their infants to be eaten before their eyes by the crocodiles in the river and on its banks. Sick and dying people are also constantly brought that they may die on its sacred shore, as they think they then reach a state of blessedness. When these sick and suffering ones are laid down by their friends upon the bank, mud and water are often forced down their throats, until they are suffocated. If any of these poor creatures should happen to live after being brought to the river, they are never received back by their friends, but are outcasts, whom no one will notice or assist."

"Dreadful! oh, how dreadful to think that such things are being done upon this beautiful earth!" exclaimed Pearl, tears of sympathy rolling down her cheeks, at but the recital of such woe. That night she thanked God anew, that they had been permitted to assist *even one* of these forsaken sufferers.

As time passed on, the careful nursing

and tender watchfulness bestowed upon little Eddie proved successful; he recovered and became a lively, intelligent little fellow, Pearl's greatest delight and pride. It was wonderful how she watched over this boy, nursing him if sick, teaching him when well, and daily praying with him, and talking to him about the nature of sin and the need of a Saviour. Eddie clung to her as he did to no one else; and seeing the influence for good which she ever exerted upon him, her friends did not interfere, but allowed him to be her own peculiar charge.

Eddie made rapid advances in learning to read the next six months, and also early manifested a childlike faith in all that was told him of the Saviour; while his obedience and gentleness soon won every heart in the mission.

Thus a year and a half passed away, when Mr. Colman received a letter from

Mrs. Lacy, saying that her health had been so far restored that she should sail for her home the next week, where the only pang that awaited her was the knowledge that she should not there meet her pastor and his wife, and her own darling Pearl. She had anticipated re-commencing house-keeping; but Ernest would not be at home much, as he intended studying for the ministry, which would deprive her of his society, except during his vacations.

Pearl was always delighted when a letter arrived from mamma Lacy, and this one especially pleased her, as it spoke so encouragingly of the health of her benefactress. Then also, was not Ernest, her almost brother, about to become a laborer for Christ! What could possibly give her deeper satisfaction! So little Pearl carried her joy to the throne of grace, and fervently thanked

God for this great mercy that he had shown her friend, in improving her health, and also for leading her son to the ministry of his holy word.

Time passed on, months gliding into years, and still Mr. Colman's family labored for the conversion of souls in that far distant land. Through their united efforts, their noble self-denials, and their fervent prayers to God for the aid of his Holy Spirit, their work was much blessed. Many, very many, having been rescued from the horrors of heathenism and made a good profession, were received into the communion of the church, and several learned men among the Hindoos became native teachers, and thus obtained great influence over the minds of the people around.

Pearl was now nearly nineteen years old, and in all this passing time she certainly had "done what she could." Several conversions were to be traced under God, to her, and still her zeal pressed her on, never allowing her to look back or to regret the course she had taken in thus giving up her country, and her former loved ones, for the sake of the destitute heathen.

During all this time her own education had not been neglected, but had received the most careful attention from Mr. Colman, who was, in every respect a superior instructor of youth. Mrs. Colman also spared no pains in imparting useful knowledge to her fondly loved child. So that now, when so many years of her life had been numbered, we find her as far advanced as most other girls of her own age, who had enjoyed the advantages of superior institutions at home.

CHAPTER X.

Changes.

ABOUT this time, in the providence of God, a dark cloud arose to mar the happiness of the mission, resulting in another change in the current of Pearl Woodford's life.

Mr. Colman, the devoted Christian, the affectionate husband, and the faithful friend, was suddenly snatched away by death.

That was a trying hour for Pearl, but nobly she bore up under the affliction, devoting all her energies to console and comfort the stricken widow, her almost mother; while kindly hands, which were immediately summoned by the frightened native servants, prepared the cold body for the silent home awaiting it.

Heart-disease, that sudden terrifying agent of death, was the cause of the hasty summons to eternity of this loved and faithful man.

Surely there were no hearts in all that station but mourned the death of Mr. Colman, for rarely had a missionary a stronger hold upon the affections of the converts than had this shepherd who had labored among them so many years. His funeral was a solemn and impressive one, and tender hands laid him peacefully to rest beneath the deep shade of the banyan-tree, in a beautiful and quiet spot within sight of his former home.

"We see thee still.
Thou art not in the grave confined;
Death cannot chain the immortal mind.
Let earth close o'er its sacred trust,
But goodness dies not in the dust.

Thee, oh, our brother, 't is not thee
Beneath the coffin's lid we see;
Thou to a fairer land art gone;
There let us hope, our journey done,
To see thee still."

From this fearful shock Mrs. Colman's rather delicate constitution could hardly rally. Though she did not murmur that this affliction had been sent to her by the will of her heavenly Father, and though she patiently bowed to the rod that had smitten her, still her strength seemed to give way, and there was an almost complete prostration of her physical powers. All suitable remedies were resorted to; journeys to the more mountainous and cooler regions were tried, but to no effect; she continued to sink perceptibly and rapidly, and at length it was announced that nothing could save her life but her immediate return to America.

This was a great blow to Mrs. Colman

and to Pearl. To leave a work in which they were so deeply interested and so much needed, was a trial indeed.

But there was no escape; and with tearful eyes and longing looks towards the never-to-be-forgotten banyan-grove they bade adieu to weeping friends around, and left for the port from which they were to embark on the stanch old ship "Sea-Bird" for their distant home.

Before they left, however, they placed little Eddie, to whom they were so much attached, in the care of a devoted missionary and his wife, who agreed to watch over him as faithfully as though they were present. The parting with this converted heathen boy was affecting, and we will only add that Pearl ever continued sending him tokens of love, money, clothing, etc., until he was thoroughly educated and became a teacher among his own people, where he labored successfully until he died at the early age of twenty-two.

After their arrival at the neighboring port, they were not long delayed before the vessel sailed; and as the beautiful shores of this Eastern land receded from sight, as the tall cocoa and Palmyra trees could be seen no more waving in the distance, they turned away to hide the tears they could not control.

Their voyage was a quiet and prosperous one. Although they met the usual gales in rounding the Cape, all was safely accomplished, and in twenty weeks they safely reached their native shores, where Mrs. Colman, in much improved health, was cordially welcomed and cared for by her own immediate relatives and friends.

On the third day after their arrival in port, Pearl was fondly clasped in the arms of Mrs. Lacy, who had come to welcome her and take her, as a daughter, to her own home; while a true brotherly welcome was extended to her by Ernest, now the dearly loved pastor of the church at Edgeville. Pearl was overjoyed at meeting these dear friends again, and she returned Mrs. Lacy's caresses with heartfelt emotion.

After the first rapture of their meeting had passed, and after a long and tender conversation had ensued, in which Mrs. Colman related to them all the particulars of her husband's death, his funeral, and his deeply-deplored loss, Mrs. Lacy told Pearl that she wished to return home as soon as possible, as Mattie was alone, and that she desired her to accompany them, as for the future she was to reside in her family.

It did not take long for Pearl to make her simple preparations; and after an affecting and affectionate farewell to Mrs. Colman, during which frequent visits were promised for this noble woman's comfort, Pearl set her face with her early friends towards the familiar scenes at Edgeville.

How quietly beautiful this lovely village looked to Pearl, as stepping from the dépôt into the waiting carriage she rode through the principal streets. On their way to Mrs. Lacy's home, they passed the neat village church, where Ernest now supplied the pulpit once occupied by Mr. Colman. The parsonage, also, where her babyhood so happily glided past, looked just as it did when they bade it that long farewell. No pastor's family resided there now, as Ernest made his home at Maple Grove with his mother and sister, while this pleasant abode was rented to a worthy family.

Pearl's reception at Maple Grove by Mattie was of the coldest character, and the young girl saw at a glance that the old animosity still ruled in her selfish, unamiable breast.

She sighed as this truth was so unpleasantly unfolded to her; but turning sadly away from the haughty young woman, she met the loving glances of her dear mamma, as Mrs. Lacy still insisted upon Pearl's calling her; and she resolved to cast the shadow of this reception from her heart, and to be happy in the affection of this valued friend and her son, even if trials should be in store for her from Mattie's unkindness. "This," said Mrs. Lacy, "is now your home; to every spot in this house my dear adopted daughter is most affectionately welcomed."

Weeks went pleasantly by to young Pearl Woodford now. To Mrs. Lacy, who was much broken in health and strength, she became a source of deepest joy. Her piety, her good sense, and her watchful affection, were so different from her own daughter's wayward stubbornness, that the wounded heart of the mother rested peacefully upon the love of her adopted child.

As Pearl was now nineteen years of age, by no means uneducated, yet lacking in some accomplishments, it was thought best by Mrs. Lacy that she should visit a superior seminary, about a mile from Maple Grove, at certain hours, to take lessons in music, French, and drawing, and in each of these branches she made rapid progress. The hours when she was not occupied were passed beside Mrs. Lacy, whom she regarded with most fervent gratitude and love.

On the Sabbath, a class of bright, intelligent little girls welcomed her with smiles to the Sunday-school room, where they listened as she spoke to them of Jesus, and related many an interesting tale of scenes she had witnessed in far-off India. Thus it may be readily seen that, although God in his holy providence had recalled her to this land, he did not take from her the love for the missionary work that had ever been hers from her earliest remembrance. She felt that, even in Edgeville, the good work could be advanced by cultivating a love for this cause in the hearts of the little ones, and this she sought prayerfully to accomplish. That she succeeded, the smiling faces with which these children welcomed her instructions and presented their little offerings at the weekly contributions, bore a cheering and decided testimony.

CHAPTER XI.

A Letter.

ONE morning after Pearl had kissed Mrs. Lacy good-by, and had mildly returned "a soft answer" to some unmerited rebuff from Mattie, and had then passed on to the seminary, a letter was brought from the postoffice to Mrs. Lacy, which she opened with wondering curiosity.

It was from Mr. Clay, her old friend, who wrote at the request of the police-officer, who years before had brought to her arms the greatest treasure, in the person of her darling Pearl. It was indeed exciting news that she soon unfolded to Ernest, and afterwards to Pearl, who hurried to her side as soon as she entered the dwelling.

To Mrs. Olive M. Lacy:

"June 20, 18—.

"My dear Friend: After the lapse of so many years, it is a great delight to me that I am at last enabled to lift the veil that has hovered strangely over the young girl you have in your charge, whose history has so long been a deep and impenetrable mystery.

"A few days since, Mr. Hardcastle the police-officer called at my store to gain some intelligence of the child he committed to your care many years ago. I told him of her safe return from India, and of her quiet prosperity at the home of her first friend.

"After this information was given, Mr. Hardcastle related to me the following circumstances, which he begged me immediately to communicate to you.

"It seems that this worthy man was startled a day or two since by receiving a telegraphic despatch, urging him to visit a certain street and number, where information of the utmost importance awaited him. I need not say that before night Mr. Hardcastle was standing before the house designated, and was, upon ringing for admission, immediately ushered into a well-furnished room, where upon a bed, pale and suffering, lay a man about fifty-five years of age. When his name was announced, he requested to be left alone with Mr. Hardcastle for a few moments, as he wished to see him upon important private business. After all had retired, he asked Mr. Hardcastle to draw his chair closer to the bedside; then in broken, faltering accents, he asked: 'Do you recollect rescuing a beautiful white female child from a vile den in the city of ——, kept by a negress?' Surprised at his recalling that never-forgotten circumstance, our honest friend replied in the affirmative.

"'Sir, you see before you a dying man; and the sin committed against that child and its sorrowing parents arises between my God and my poor soul, and I must confess and make every reparation I can, before I go to that 'bourne from which no traveller returns.' But before I go farther, answer me one question to relieve my anxiety. Does that child still live?

"'She does,' he answered; 'and from all I can learn, she is a beautiful, amiable, and pious young girl, now about nineteen years of age.'

"'Thank God for that! Then, when restored to her still mourning parents, she will prove a blessing instead of a curse as I so long intended. Years ago, I loved the mother of that child, and sought by every means to win her affections and her consent to become my wife, in vain. She despised me, and married finally the one to whom alone she gave her pure, young heart. He was a noble young man, good, benevolent, and fine-looking, from a family of wealth and high standing; and this Christian couple are still living. You start, but my story is true. Horace Dunbarton is the father of the child you rescued, and whom I stole out of a cruel revenge for the disregard paid to my love for its beautiful mother.

"'Yes; I stole that infant from its cradle, where the nurse had left it sleeping quietly a few moments before; and without being seen or suspected, I hurried with it in my arms to a carriage I had in waiting, and escaped to the house of Molly Clarkson, a negress I had hired to assist me in my villany. Once in her hands, I was sure its parents would never trace it, nor have they. To this day they have never heard one word of their idolized babe.'

"Here the sick man became nearly suffocated by a fearful turn of coughing, which seemed to prostrate even the remnant of strength remaining, and some time elapsed before he could give the particular address of the parents, in the city of ———, which I now hasten to enclose to you. Mr. Hardcastle promised the dying man that he would immediately communicate the intelligence to you, and through you, to those parents who so long have been left in suspense as to the fate of their child; and by his request I have written this statement.

"I have never forgotten to feel interested in the welfare of little Pearl; and it is with deep joy that I write this intelligence.

"I will only add that the poor, sinful man died the night after that interview.

"Thanking you for your benevolence and kindness in the past, I close.

"Yours respectfully,
"HARLAND M. CLAY."

So our friend Pearl was no longer Pearl Woodford the unknown, but Blanche Dunbarton, the daughter of a well-known and respected gentleman. It was strange how this knowledge allayed Miss Mattie Lacy's animosity, and what airs of external respect she immediately assumed towards the one she had treated with insult and disdain.

But such was the case. Mattie was like many others in this calculating world, hard and oppressive to those considered beneath them, but fawning and wily to the rich and lofty.

Conclusion.

TIME will not permit me to follow Pearl to the joyful moment when she was folded to the hearts of her own father and mother, to whom she was immediately taken by the affectionate hands of Mrs. Lacy and Ernest. The meeting was most affecting; many tears were shed, and many thanks offered during that tender and joyful interview.

At length, at the earnest request of Pearl, as we must still continue to call her, she was permitted to return for a time to Mrs. Lacy, whose health had been very poor for many months, and who was hardly yet reconciled to parting with one so dear as her adopted daughter.

Mrs. Lacy did not linger long before she was seized with a severe stroke of paralysis; and with her hands clasped fondly by Ernest and Pearl, she quietly fell asleep in Jesus, passing through the dark valley without much apparent suffering; and though mourned by a wide circle of friends, it was with the knowledge that death to her was indescribable gain.

We must now leave our young friend, having followed her thus far on life's journey, and having seen the commencement of a course of Christian life which she followed to the very end. Not the least, in our estimation, of her works of piety, was the faithful return she made her adopted mother for all her kindness to her. It is grateful to think how she soothed and filled the heart wounded and desolate through the coldness and disobedience of an only daughter, and how she cheered her in her last hours.

We leave her, then, restored to her own parents, to whom she became very soon deeply attached, and with whom she spent some happy years, until her adopted brother Ernest followed her to her distant abode, where they renewed their friendship. Then as Mrs. Ernest Lacy she once more entered upon missionary work, but this time upon the soil of her native country, in the capacity of the loving, faithful wife of a devoted pastor. Ever fervent, ever bright had been her missionary spirit; and though she never returned to India's benighted land, she still found ample scope for doing the Master's work among the destitute and ignorant upon her own native shores.

www.ingramcontent.com/pod-product-compliance
Lightning Source LLC
Chambersburg PA
CBHW031122160426
43192CB00008B/1081